C000018816

THE LIFE & TIMES OF
WOLFGANG AMADEUS MOZART

THE LIFE & TIMES OF

Wolfgang Amadeus Mozart

BY
A. Noble

This edition printed for, Shooting Star Press Inc, 230
Fifth Avenue, Suite 1212, New York, NY 10001

Shooting Star Press books are available at special discount
for bulk purchases for sales promotions, premiums, fund-
raising or educational use. Special editions or book
excerpts can also be created to specification. For details
contact – Special Sales Director, Shooting Star Press Inc.,
230 Fifth Avenue, Suite 1212, New York, NY 10001

This edition first published by Parragon Books
Produced by Magpie Books Ltd, 7 Kensington Church
Court, London W8 4SP
Copyright © Parragon Book Service Ltd 1994
Illustrations courtesy of: Mary Evans Picture Library.

ISBN 1 57335 036 2
A copy of the British Library Cataloguing in Publication
Data is available from the British Library.

Typeset by Hewer Text Composition Services, Edinburgh
Printed in Singapore by Printlink International Co.

Introduction

1756. To most people this is a year of little significance. A few may know that it was the year the Seven Years War started. Fewer still may be able to name some of the personalities involved, such as Frederick the Great or Pitt the Elder or General Wolfe. But almost everybody has heard of Mozart, even if they didn't know he was born in 1756.

Most of his contemporaries have disappeared into the mists of history; their importance at the time, their achievements, now forgotten.

But Mozart's name lives on. The reasons for this are simple: he wrote music that people still love to hear and play, music that still moves people as much as it did over 200 years ago. His music is used as theme tunes on the television and radio. So we have all heard it even if we did not realise it was Mozart. Films have been made of his most popular operas, *The Magic Flute* and *Don Giovanni*. And what other composer could have been the subject himself of a popular film – *Amadeus*? Mozart had such miraculous ability that he still fascinates scholars and playwrights.

He was one of the supreme geniuses in Western art, working in a medium that affects people as no other art form does. Why music works on the emotions so, when it is such an ephemeral, passing experience is hard to explain, but nobody would deny that it does. And Mozart was lucky: he was born at a time when the work of composers was beginning to reach a wider audience – not just the preserve of kings, the nobility and the rich – and at a time when music was finding new freedom of expression. Like all geniuses, he was an innovator and could turn old forms to new uses. Nevertheless, it is fortunate for us that he was born when the rigid mathematical formality of composers' work was falling out of favour. J. S. Bach, for example, wrote pieces which were based on words with the letters providing the notes (i.e. a 'C' would be represented by middle 'C' on the piano). Nowadays, such artistic games are mostly laughed at as being too artificial.

In the late eighteenth century composers and musicians were regarded in a very different way from how they are now. If they were extremely lucky they held positions such as *Kapellmeister* (chapel or church master), where they were in charge of organising the music for all the religious ceremonies, or *Cantor* where they were in charge of the choir. The holders of such positions were expected to compose music as well as organise the orchestras and choirs and whatever else was required. Alternatively, they might work for an aristocratic patron, who might pay them a decent salary. But not all aristocrats loved music and even fewer were prepared to pay for it. This made such positions scarce. They also tended to regard 'their' composers as servants: one of Mozart's most famous contemporaries, Joseph Haydn, worked virtually all his life for the Esterhazy family; while they treated him well enough he was always at their beck and call and had to write what they required of him, be it a symphony, a concerto, a mass or an opera. On the staff scale he was probably regarded as being somewhere between a personal valet – a gentleman's gentleman – and the domestics. And when one's patron died, one might well be out of a job if his successor did not share his tastes. Life was very uncertain.

This was the world into which Mozart was born.

Prodigy on Display

In the eighteenth century, Germany was divided into many states and principalities, some of which were quite large, like Prussia, Bavaria and Saxony, but most of which were tiny, consisting of barely more than one medium-sized town. These either passed down through families or were handed out by the church. One of the latter was Catholic Salzburg where the prince was also the archbishop. Salzburg was very much a backwater, conservative and fervently anti-Protestant.

Leopold Mozart, Wolfgang's father, was a musician-servant at the court of Prince Archbishop Siegmund Christoph von Schrattenbach (ruler 1753-1771), playing in the court orchestra. He was highly competent: at the time of Wolfgang's birth, 27 January 1756, he was writing a textbook on violin playing and by 1763 he had been promoted to *Vizekapellmeister* at the court.

Wolfgang was born into a small family; he was only the second survivor out of six children and his mother nearly died giving birth to him. The other was his sister, born in 1751, Maria Anna Walburga Ignatia, known as 'Nannerl'. She was a musical child and was able to play the clavier (a small harpsichord) well. When Wolfgang arrived, Leopold had high hopes that he would be able to nurture another excellent musician. He could have had no idea how much his hopes would be exceeded.

Almost immediately Wolfgang showed his precocity. At the age of four he wrote a clavier concerto. The paper it was written on was so covered with infantile scrawl, blots and mess, that Leopold at first thought nothing of it. He then managed to decipher it. The notes seemed too hard to play, but Wolfgang then astonished his father by being able to play it, while explaining it was a concerto.

The Mozart family seems to have been a reasonably happy one. There was music almost all the time – Wolfgang even liked to move his toys from room to room to the accompaniment of mock musical marches – and the family enjoyed jokes, crude humour and horseplay. Leopold clearly loved Wolfgang and wanted to expand his musical horizons. There was a vogue at the time for so-called 'exotic' music – 'Turkish' and 'Chinese' (nothing of the sort in reality, it

8

consisted mostly of using odd instruments and scoring, neither of which had anything to do with the real thing). Leopold made sure Wolfgang heard these 'foreign' styles of music, as well as taking him to an opera before he was seven. Sometimes he was rather hard on the boy, though, in his urgency to educate him, as when he blew a trumpet directly at Wolfgang to overcome his aversion to the instrument. Not many teachers would recommend this approach now.

As soon as he could, Leopold wanted to display the skills of his son. It was an era when child prodigies frequently performed, as curiosities. And so, in 1762, the Mozarts visited the Elector Maximilian III Joseph in Munich. The Elector himself may have been absent, but Wolfgang and Nannerl seem to have performed successfully for the court. The family then left for Vienna: en route they stayed at Linz – later to give its name to Mozart's 36th Symphony – where Wolfgang gave his first public concert on 3 October 1762. It seems to have received great applause. In any event, a nobleman who happened to be passing through, Count Palffy, was present. He spoke of the prodigy to the Archduke Joseph who mentioned him to his mother, the Empress Maria Theresa. The Mozarts were then summoned to the Imperial Palace at Schönbrunn. They spent three hours with the Empress and her family, which was a clear sign of imperial favour.

Wolfgang began a punishing series of performances that enchanted his audiences. In Vienna he showed his musical brilliance by such tricks as covering the keyboard with a cloth while still playing correctly and accurately identifying the notes of bells and clocks. He also improvised. But the six-year-old found public playing exhausting:

although he was totally absorbed in the music and loved to play, he developed a rash which was thought to be scarlet fever, widespread in Vienna at the time. Luckily, he was cured quite quickly.

The young players – Nannerl performed as well – were extremely popular. Being small, the children seemed younger than they in fact were and this added to their appeal. When it was time to leave, the Imperial Chancellor, Kaunitz, wanted the Mozarts to stay longer, while the French Ambassador invited the family to Versailles. In early 1763 the family returned to Salzburg where Wolfgang was extremely ill, probably with rheumatism, an ailment that dogged him through his life and which may have shortened it.

On 9 June 1763 the family set off on another tour, one which was to last for three years.

The young Mozart

Mozart's mother Maria

They criss-crossed Germany, playing in the palaces of the petty princes, before reaching Paris on 18 November. Paris was regarded as the centre of European culture, though in 1763 it was no longer at its best, France having just lost the Seven Years War. The Mozarts received a grand reception and met several well-known German composers. Wolfgang had his first works published here, two *Sonates pur le Clavecin* (Sonatas for the Clavier/Harpsichord) which came out in March 1764.

This should have been an important step for Wolfgang, as publishing was one of the only means of getting one's work more widely known. Home music-making was a major form of entertainment for middle-class and aristocratic families, and the only access most of them had to it was through works specially written or arranged for small groups. But this was something of a flash in the pan, and

Wolfgang had very little of his mature work published. In any event, a composer did not keep the copyright to his work, receiving only a one-off payment. And if he was not already well-known, this would not amount to much.

The family then moved on to London in 1764: here again, it was received well. George III had recently come to the throne and was a great music-lover, especially of Handel, and very much enjoyed the young Mozart's playing of his music. Also in England public concerts were well-established, giving Leopold plenty of opportunity to earn money through his gifted children. After Paris, the lack of artificiality of English behaviour was a welcome relief, and despite complaints about the weather, the family stayed there for 15 months, longer than at any other place on their tours.

More important though, with the Hanover-
ian kings, there was a strong German influence in London, and there were many
German composers and musicians there,
including Johann Christian Bach (a son of
Johann Sebastian Bach). Bach was beginning
to move away from rigid formal structures in
his symphonies and strongly influenced
Mozart, who went on to produce his First
Symphony (K. 16) in London. He also
published six sonatas dedicated to Queen
Charlotte. The family eventually left in July
1765. Before they departed Mozart presented a motet to the British Museum.

They arrived in Calais on 1 August 1765,
and after the relative calm of London – at
least they were not constantly on the move –
life became really hectic again. They started
with Holland, then moved on to Paris,
Versailles, Dijon, Lyons, Geneva and Lau-
sanne. Travelling in the eighteenth century

was an uncomfortable experience; the roads were bad – one could only really do between 15 and 20 miles a day – carriages were not particularly well-protected from the weather or well-sprung and every night one would be staying at a different inn, all of which must have been hard on a nine-year-old. Not surprisingly, both Mozart and Nannerl fell ill from exhaustion, both catching typhoid. They then travelled on into Germany, reaching Munich, where Mozart suffered seriously from rheumatism again. This extended tour finally came to an end in November 1766. It had been a triumphant success, with Mozart attracting praise and attention wherever he went; receiving presents from royalty and congratulatory reviews.

Budding Composer

After the excitement of his years on the road, Mozart's life reverted to tranquillity. His days as an infant prodigy were effectively over; he was now eleven and it became more important for him to begin a career as a composer. The first potential opportunity for him to publicly display his composing skills was the impending marriage of King Ferdinand of Naples and the Archduchess Josepha in Vienna. Leopold clearly hoped that his son would be commissioned to write some celebratory pieces. Unfortunately, that

autumn there was an outbreak of small pox
in Vienna. The Archduchess caught it and
died; the celebrations were clearly off. Nannerl and Mozart both had milder attacks. It
then appeared that the Emperor Joseph II
wanted to commission an opera from Mozart
but this was thwarted by the manager of the
two main theatres in Vienna. The family
returned to Salzburg in January 1769.

Mozart had actually written an opera for the
expected commission, *La Finta Semplice* (The
Feigned Innocent), and this was performed
once for the Prince-Archbishop's name day.
La Finta Semplice was a step forward for
Mozart, and was the first of his operas to
feature a soubrette, a pert and humorous
chambermaid. Schrattenbach was clearly
well-disposed towards the Mozarts, father
and son, and encouraged Wolfgang to pro-
vide more compositions. This he did with
fluency; Leopold kept a list of his son's

compositions, noting at the end of this period in Salzburg that they amounted to 558 pages.

The work included the full range of musical types: divertimenti (short pieces written almost as background entertainment), symphonies, two masses, an oratorio and a *Singspiel* (a musical play, specifically written for German audiences, with the dialogue in German) called *Bastien und Bastienne*. This *Singspiel* does not seem to have greatly inspired Mozart: the plot centres on two children, and as a thirteen-year-old, he probably wanted to write about more adult topics.

Leopold was highly ambitious for his son, and thought that he should be exposed to Italian music, especially opera, as Italy was the leading nation in this field. He petitioned Schrattenbach for leave from his post at

ot only was this granted but Schrat-
gave the Mozarts money for the trip
ointed Wolfgang his third concert-
Although the post was unpaid, it was
honour for one so young and gave
tus at court.

o, in January 1770, father and son
d off for Italy. This was a period of
excitement for Mozart as there were
ent visits to the opera. Italy was ex-
ely hospitable to the Mozarts, and
lfgang frequently performed to great
plause. Wolfgang also made new friends,
ne of whom was an English violin virtuoso
f his own age. He also had to speak Italian,
which was very useful, considering that most
of his operas would use Italian rather than
German. Soon Wolfgang received his first
commission, an *opera seria*, to be called
Mitridate, Re di Ponte (Mithridates, King of
Pontus). Opera was divided into two kinds at

Wolfgang Amadeus with his father and sister

View of Salzburg in Mozart's time

the time: *opera seria* was, as the name implies, about serious subjects, often loosely based on Classical history, as in the case of Mitridate, or Classical myths; *opera buffa* was comic opera. *Mitridate* was to be performed at the Milan opera house at the end of the year. Mozart took his work so calmly that he was still writing the main characters' parts only a month before the first performance was due. Here, as throughout his career, he wrote music to suit specific voices; the lead singer was Benedetti, a castrato, and Mozart waited until he had arrived before writing his part. He stated that he did not want to have to do the work twice, in the event that the music and the voice did not suit.

The opera turned out to be a triumphant success: Mozart was received into the Accademia Filharmonica, a prestigious musical society, on 9 October 1770, where the rules had to be suspended to allow in a member less than twenty years old. The Pope also made him a Knight of the Golden Spur, a title Mozart never used except occasionally in jest. The newspapers praised *Mitridate* literally to the stars – *alle stelle* – and the opera had to be copied out for the court in Lisbon, and sent to Vienna and Parma. Mozart was dubbed '*il Signor Cavaliere Filharmonico*' by the Italians – Sir Music-lover. Finally, on the strength of the opera, Mozart received a commission to write a *festa teatrale* – a theatrical celebration – for the marriage in Milan of Maria Theresa's third son, the Archduke Ferdinand, in autumn 1771.

Leopold and Wolfgang returned to Salzburg in January 1771, Wolfgang now with an extraordinary reputation for one so young. They were not there long: they returned to Milan for the Archduke's wedding, for which Mozart had composed *Ascanio in Alba*. It was a typical light festive piece, though because the Archduke's bride was not particularly attractive, there were none of the usual hymns to beauty. The Archduke liked it sufficiently to propose to his mother that Mozart be hired by the court. She had firm views about not hiring 'useless people' among whom she counted composers, and nothing came of it. Nonetheless, while Mozart was in Milan he received two more opera commissions, for Milan itself and for Venice, to be completed the following year.

Leopold also wrote to the music publisher Breitkopf, in Leipzig, in the hope that he might publish Mozart's work. Leopold promised that Mozart could write any piece Breitkopf might care to order. In a sign of things to come, he did not even receive a reply. It may seem extraordinary to us now, but most of Mozart's work was probably only heard once, if at all, during his lifetime.

A Taste of Independence

On 14 March 1772, Schrattenbach, the music-loving, supportive Prince-Arch-bishop, died. His successor, Hieronymus Count Colloredo, is now known for only one thing: he was the man who quarrelled with and ultimately dismissed Mozart from court service. In retrospect this seems to have been a good thing. Salzburg was notoriously small-minded and philistine – Mozart de-scribed audiences there as no better than tables and chairs – very wooden. His frustration must have been due in part to the fact that he was discovering his own individuality as a composer and his artistic independence. That he escaped a stifling environment, even if half-unwillingly, was to the world's benefit, if not his own financially.

But he was not idle during his last period in Salzburg. It was a composer's role to produce music to order. Art in general was seen as a form of entertainment as much as of instruction. The Romantic notion, which we have held virtually since the turn of the nineteenth century, that art is an end in itself, was not recognized in Mozart's time (and there are indications that it is being questioned now). One of his own favourite music forms was the dance – he liked to write music for movement, which shows his zest for life and the absence of self-importance in his character. Even in the last year of his life he was very pleased to discover that a tune from

The Marriage of Figaro had been rearranged for dancing. Furthermore, he had inherited a love of humour in music from Leopold who had written some quite absurd pieces, including scoring for sleighbells and whips. Mozart produced many divertimenti, serenades and nocturnes. Serenades were to celebrate special occasions or impress one's loved one and nocturnes were simply gentle pieces to be played in the evening. Music to relax to, to chat through, not music approached in the hushed reverent manner of the modern concert hall.

During 1772 he also wrote eight symphonies: these are light, enjoyable pieces, little more in some cases than serenades. Nonetheless they were the longest non-vocal pieces he had written so far. He wrote these virtually for himself: after the success of *Ascanio* and with his two opera commissions, he could afford to spend time compos-

Mozart with his Sonata No. 8

An eighteenth century chamber concert

ing on the off-chance that Breitkopf might publish them. Many influences have been detected in these symphonies, for example, those of C. P. E. Bach and Joseph Haydn. But already Mozart was showing that he could compose with more variety than his contemporaries, and in these symphonies he began to experiment with painting different moods which go way beyond the limited expressiveness of other composers of the time. Even in formal works such as *Il Sogno di Scipione* (The Dream of Scipio), written to celebrate Colloredo's election, he showed an ability to match the music to the seriousness of the script.

In late October 1772, he and Leopold left again for Italy. He had a two-month deadline within which to complete his commission for Milan, the opera *Lucio Silla*. Even with the first night only three weeks off he still had fourteen numbers to compose and then, when at the last moment the leading tenor had to be replaced, he was left with only four days to write the new tenor's. *Lucio Silla* was very successful and highly praised but received only a few performances after its première on 26 December, not being performed again till modern times.

Apart from this success, this second trip to Italy turned out to be rather dull. Leopold Mozart tried in vain to get a post for Wolfgang with the Archduke Leopold of Tuscany, just as he had failed with Ferdinand the previous year. In many ways Mozart's father was unable to see that times were beginning to change, and that working in the employ of aristocratic patrons was slowly ceasing to be the best course for an ambitious artist.

The next trip abroad was to Vienna, where Leopold and Wolfgang travelled as part of

Colloredo's entourage, in July 1773. The two Mozarts remained there after the Prince-Archbishop had left. For Wolfgang, it was an interesting time. He met the Mesmer family (one of whom gave the word 'mesmerize' to the language), who were highly musical and closely involved in the world of theatre, a combination of interests that Wolfgang shared. He also wrote a group of six quartets, his third, now known as the 'Vienna' Quartets, which clearly show the influence of Haydn. These quartets were almost certainly written for pleasure, for private performance by the composer with professional or amateur musician friends.

When they returned to Salzburg at the end of September, life was really dull – no kindred spirits, no commissions, apart from the incidental music to *Thamos, King of Egypt*, a rather silly play. It was not until the end of 1774 that a commission arrived for an *opera buffa*. This was to become *La Finta Gardiniera* (The Feigned Gardener[ess]) and was Mozart's first opera success north of the Alps. It had been commissioned by the Bavarian Elector, Maximilian III Joseph, who loved it, bravoing loudly, with his wife, at the first performance. The Bishop of Chiemsee sent him a note congratulating him. Unfortunately, only two more performances were given and Mozart lost interest in it. He was not to realise that this would be his last proper opera commission for five years.

La Finta Gardiniera has a farcical plot, with the heroine disguising herself as a gardener in order to pursue her cruel lover. It is not particularly funny, it has a pointlessly complicated plot and the characters are not very pleasant. What it does demonstrate, though, are signs of the mature Mozart, as here he showed his ability to intertwine the music and the drama – most operas of the time were rather static, with lots of set numbers, even Gluck's (a leading contemporary composer, now being re-evaluated), despite the latter's declared intent to fuse drama and music. Mozart actually achieved this fusion.

The only person not sharing in the general applause was Colloredo, who managed to avoid attending any of the performances and who was clearly embarrassed, despite the Mozarts being in his service, when Maximilian III congratulated him on its success. It was quite clear that Colloredo was beginning to dislike the Mozarts; their prolonged leaves of absence almost certainly did not help. The Mozarts returned to Salzburg, as unwilling servants, to endure what threatened to be a sterile period. Virtually the only commission in 1775 was for a *serenata*, in this case a short opera written for the entertainment of Maria

Theresa's youngest son, the Archduke Max-imilian, on a visit to Salzburg. By general consensus it is a conventional and dull piece.

Unable to suppress his innate creativity, Mozart began to write instrumental concer-tos and symphonies; it was at this time that he wrote his first piano concerto (K 175); this shows his musical emancipation from Haydn and the *Sturm und Drang* movement in Germany, where artists were supposed to give vent to extreme and sentimental feel-ings. Mozart performed this piano concerto on several occasions and was clearly fond of it because eight years later he gave it a new third movement (K 382). It was during this year, too, that he wrote the five violin concertos (others have been attributed to him but their authenticity is still disputed). He had developed a strong interest in the violin at the time, and was a good performer. More of an incentive, perhaps, for writing the series was that his father played the violin, as did Colloredo, and the first violinist in the latter's orchestra was known to be excellent. He also wrote for local amateurs a piano concerto (K 246) and the concerto for three pianos (K 242).

In 1776 he composed the well-known 'Haffner' Serenade (K 250) for Elizabeth Haffner, the burgomaster of Salzburg's daughter. This is a serious piece despite being written for a celebratory occasion. But Mozart was growing increasingly bored with Salzburg; the court did not show any particular interest in music and writing quartets or church music was mostly for his own amusement. Colloredo also imposed constraints on what could be written for the church – for example, he banned fugues, and masses had to be no longer than three-quarters of an hour. Mozart got round this last restriction by compressing some parts to a minimum – barely time to say the words – so as to give himself room in the sections where he wanted to develop his themes.

Eventually in 1777 Mozart petitioned to be discharged from Colloredo's service. To his and Leopold's surprise, both of them were sacked. Leopold became ill with fright and cravenly begged to be reinstated. He was taken back into service, but thereafter felt unable to leave Salzburg. His control over his son's career was effectively at an end and could only be exercised at a distance.

On 23 September 1777, as winter was drawing in, Mozart and his mother left Salzburg in search of a post for him. They progressed to Munich where there were no vacancies. In Augsburg he was met by complete indifference and rudeness, though he managed to squeeze in a brief flirtation with his cousin, from which some rather earthy correspondence has survived. Mannheim seemed better; it was famous for its composers – there was even a 'Mannheim Group', now largely forgotten.

Its Elector, Karl Theodor, was a patron of the arts and wanted to produce opera that was German rather than Italian. Mozart played for him and the Elector gave him a watch! Mozart also encountered the Weber family, old friends from previous tours. Mozart promptly fell in love with the eldest daughter Aloysia, for whom he wished to write an opera to show off her singing ability. He grew to like the whole Weber family – they provided a home from home. In such pleasant circumstances, even if not being paid well, it is not surprising that Mozart lingered in Mannheim. Leopold was furious when he heard of Wolfgang's delay as he desperately wanted him to actively pursue finding a court position. It was clear, too, that he did not like the fact that Wolfgang was now independent of him; in the past they had always travelled together. A voluminous correspondence of advice and demands followed Wolfgang from Salzburg, though he does not seem to have been too affected by them. In the new year, Maximilian III Joseph of Bavaria died and was succeeded by Karl Theodor. This seemed a heaven-sent opportunity, as Karl Theodor would become much wealthier and more powerful, but nothing came of it.

Leopold constantly urged Mozart to go to Paris and eventually he set off with his mother. But Paris was not the town it had been. Rousseau and Voltaire, two of the most influential French thinkers of the eighteenth century, both died in 1778. The new king, Louis XVI, was a singularly uninspiring monarch, virtually silent at council meetings, and no great patron of the arts. The French

Mozart and Constanze on their honeymoon

W.A. MOZART.

Mozart with his house in Salzburg

showed their appreciation of him by guillo-
tining him in January 1793. Mozart composed the 'Paris' Symphony (K 297) which
was well-received. The trouble was that
French enthusiasm for his work was super-
ficial and was not matched in money terms.

While in Paris his mother fell ill and quickly
died. Typical of Mozart's sensitivity, though,
was that he did not immediately tell his father
that Frau Mozart had died. He prepared him
for it gradually by saying that the illness had
taken a dangerous turn – even though she
was already dead at the time he wrote this –
before letting him know the worst later.
Mozart was now completely alone, as
friends he and his father had made on their
previous visit proved distant. He had to
contemplate the unpleasant prospect of returning to Salzburg.

Coincidentally, Colloredo was in need of a

ister. Since his row with Mo-
been widely advised that it had
ous mistake to sack somebody so
And so he invited him to return and
reluctantly agreed. However, he was
hurry. He left Paris in September but
until Christmas to even reach Munich.
re he met the Webers again as they had
tled there, Herr Weber having received a
vell-paid position from Karl Theodor. Here
a shock awaited Mozart. Aloysia was no
longer interested in him (in 1780 she was
to marry an actor, Joseph Lange: in later life –
she far outlived Mozart – she was to admit
that she had been incapable of recognizing
his qualities and talents). Mozart, ever-sensi-
tive, was extremely hurt by this rejection. He
made his way back to Salzburg in early 1779,
where he was taken back into service as an
organist. It must have been extremely de-
pressing for someone so independent-
minded to find himself dragged back to

the place he had sought to escape, the place
that represented everything dull and wrong
with the world, especially after his early
exposure to so many more exciting cities
and countries. He was not to know it, but
two years of such a straitened environment
lay before him.

The Break with Salzburg

Mozart was productive in these years: he wrote several pieces that are still familiar – the 'Posthorn' Serenade (K 320), the 'Coronation' Mass (K 317), numerous symphonies and church works, and the *Sinfonia Concertante* (K 364) for violin and viola. With these pieces, Mozart began to truly find his musical character, to become the mature composer, the Mozart we recognize now. The *Sinfonia Concertante* in particular is a sublime piece, full of emotional strength,

Composing *Don Giovanni*

Illustration to *Don Giovanni*

somewhat pensive, a piece that ranks with other great works for strings such as Bach's Double Concerto, Brahms' Violin Concerto or Dvorak's Cello Concerto.

At this time Mozart came into more frequent personal contact with Haydn: he was perhaps the only person whose views Mozart really respected. He knew that the praise of audiences and critics, the cheers and bravos, were short-lived, but Haydn's views were those of a master, and he recognized Mozart as unique. Leopold was also lucky enough to meet Haydn and hear his high opinion of his son. Haydn was to describe Mozart's work as profound, musically intelligent and extraordinarily sensitive.

Wolfgang's year away from Leopold, in Mannheim and Paris, had helped him form his own views on the future of opera. In both towns he had attended plays and now began to talk of 'duodramas', a fusion of music and drama, that represented a move away from traditional *opera seria* and *opera buffa*. Leopold, conservative, was not keen on the idea as he preferred the old set pieces to a more natural style. Wolfgang also wanted to get away from the concentration on classical themes for operas: his own experience of poor playwrights and librettists (witness *Thamos*) led to him to want to control his librettists tightly, so that music and words worked perfectly together.

Towards the end of 1780 a commission arrived from Karl Theodor in Munich, for an opera *Idomeneo, Re di Creta* (Idomeneo, King of Crete), to be premiered in January 1781. Munich is not that far from Salzburg, and Mozart set off with a short leave of absence from Colloredo, probably expecting to return in the new year. But his absence this time was to prove permanent, apart from one visit to his father.

In *Idomeneo*, Mozart took a strong interest in the text. As initially presented, it was repetitive and dull: he was ruthless in cutting it. It is still long, compared to what he had written before, but at least it makes some dramatic sense, and it is successful in portraying emotions. It was also one of his two operas to introduce a supernatural element (the other was *Don Giovanni*). The première was on 29 January 1781; it proved a resounding success, and probably gave Mozart confidence in his ability to go it alone.

Shortly after the premiere Colloredo summoned Mozart to Vienna, where he resumed his friendship with the Mesmers. But Colloredo treated him capriciously, having him play in his ancient father's house and refusing him permission to perform at charity concerts. Tempers rose; Mozart hated being treated like a servant. Things came to a

head over a trivial incident: Mozart was
asked to take a package back to Salzburg
on Wednesday 9 May. It came out that
Mozart had decided not to leave till the
Saturday. Colloredo was witheringly patron-
ising, and Mozart was sarcastic in return.
Resignation was the only option. He was
in the right place, as he saw Vienna as a
centre of opportunity. At the last of several
arguments over resignation, Mozart was
actually kicked by Count Arco, Colloredo's
steward. This was the last straw.

Mozart moved in with the Webers, who had
now moved to Vienna. He received little
work there – the teaching and the opera
commissions he had hoped for did not
materialize. In the meantime he received
increasingly unpleasant letters from Leopold
who was both terrified of upsetting Colloredo and adamant in wanting Mozart to
observe his wishes. He accused Mozart of

not loving him. There was compensation, though, in his growing affection for Constanze Weber, whom he would later marry. He received the libretto for an opera *Belmont und Constanze* which would later be called *Die Entführung aus dem Serail* (The Abduction from the Harem). He then rushed to complete *Die Entführung* for a visit to Vienna by the Grand Duke Paul of Russia, but instead Gluck's *Alceste* was put on. Eventually, it was premièred on 16 July 1782, almost a year later.

The opera is a comedy, but neither purely comic nor too serious – more a reflection of real life and real feelings. Mozart, as was now his practice, had a close hand in the text: the original author Bretzner did not initially like what Mozart had done but came to recognize his genius. The story involves issues of slavery and freedom, which Mozart probably related closely to his experiences of Salzburg.

It mocks the figures of authority that Mozart had grown to despise. The Viennese loved it: Gluck asked for a repeat performance, and it was played many times over the following years. It also went on to be performed in Prague, Bonn, Hamburg, Warsaw and Weimar. *Die Entführung* made Mozart famous, if not rich. The Austrian Emperor Joseph II even believed it was his first opera; it was at a performance that he made his famous comment that he liked it but that there were too many notes – to which Mozart's reply was that there were exactly as many as were needed.

The Emperor's approval was not worth much, though; he was still wedded to the now-outdated Italian styles of opera and preferred Salieri's work to that of the real stars – Gluck, Haydn and Mozart (Salieri was court composer and director of the opera). It was not till 1787 that Mozart received a

Silhouette of Mozart

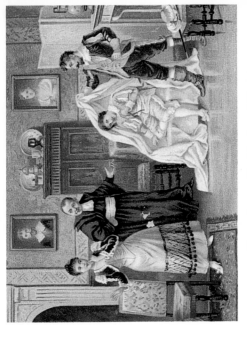

Illustration to *The Marriage of Figaro*

court position, *Kammermusikus* (chamber musician), and it only brought in a measly salary of 800 florins. Mozart's income at this time was very uncertain: he earned some money from subscriptions for printed works, some from pupils and some from public concerts. But often he had to beg from friends and patrons, as in 1783 when he was threatened with a lawsuit for an unpaid loan (and at the time one could go to prison for such an offence).

For his public performances Mozart concentrated on the piano. His was specially adapted with a large pedal board to give it more volume (the piano was in an early stage of its development and was nothing like as powerful as the concert grands, Steinways for example, that we hear now). The Piano Concertos in F major (K 413), A major (K 414) and C major (K 415) were written for subscription concerts. They are on a relatively small scale, with much of the eighteenth century in them, pretty and formal. He also wrote concertos for his pupils. For Barbara Ployer he wrote two in 1784, the second of which, No. 17, in G major (K 453), marks a significant change in scale. No longer consciously attempting to please an audience, in the sense of giving them what they expect to hear, as for the subscription concerts, Mozart put much more emotion into the concertos, and developed his authentic style. This is particularly true of the D minor, No. 20 (K 466), which in its opening chords seems to anticipate Beethoven.

Meanwhile Constanze had their first child, a son. Mozart initially told Leopold that the baby would have his name as godfather, but unfortunately also told his friend Baron Raymundl von Wetzlar who proposed himself, so the child was christened Raymundl.

This attempt to smooth family relations thus backfired. Nonetheless, Mozart and Constanze left Vienna in July 1783 to visit Leopold, not returning until October, by which time the baby had died.

Mozart was probably uncomfortable back in Salzburg, with Colloredo lurking in the background. Even so he had written most of the great C minor Mass (K 427), and Constanze believed in later years that it was performed during this visit, with herself as one of the soloists. Although incomplete – whether through subsequent loss or not – it displays immense majesty, and great intensity of feeling, in a manner hitherto unattempted. The soaring *Jesu* of the Gloria (Part II) is particularly affecting. We know that Mozart was now familiar with the works of J. S. Bach and, probably, with those of G. F Handel. Was he familiar with the B minor Mass and the *Messiah*? Whatever, the work is much more dense and passionate than what had gone before.

When he left Salzburg after this visit, he was never to return. He went to Linz, where he had been invited by Count Johann Thun-Hohenstein, whose family he had met in Vienna. Mozart arrived on 30 October with a commitment to write a symphony for a public concert by 11 November! He had nothing with him that was suitable and so – extremely quickly – wrote his Symphony No. 36 (K 425), aptly known as the 'Linz'. It marks a major change in his symphonic style, being the first to start with a slow movement and with much greater orchestral weight than its predecessors.

On his return to Vienna, Mozart's life became extremely hectic. He was giving concerts on average twice a week (nineteen alone in March 1784). He moved apartments, as he was to do twice in 1784, so as to match his income to his expenditure. In September 1784 a second son, Karl Thomas, was born, and this event probably added to his worries. Not surprisingly he was seriously ill and was probably only saved through the efforts of his friend and physician, Siegmund Barisani. At the end of the year he moved into a large apartment overlooking the Schulerstrasse, where he was to stay for three years. This flat was large and roomy – Mozart even had his own study.

The flat was host to illustrious visitors. When Leopold arrived in January 1785 for his last visit, he met Haydn who told him, 'Your son is the greatest composer I know in person or name.' Mozart obviously reciprocated this esteem, and dedicated a group of six quartets, composed from 1782 to 1785, to Haydn, '*Al mio caro amico*' – to my dear friend. Haydn had been a great inspiration to Mozart in writing quartets; he had greatly developed the form to give the instruments (two violins, a viola and a cello) their individual voices and to exploit the interplay of their different tones more effectively. It was with Haydn that the quartet ceased to be just a vehicle for private music-making and became a means of expressing one's innermost thoughts.

Lorenzo da Ponte was another visitor, now famous as Mozart's highly talented librettist. Da Ponte was interested in a collaboration. Mozart had some reservations, as da Ponte had arrived from Dresden hoping to replace Metastasio as the imperial poet, which would have involved writing libretti for Salieri. But at the same time, Mozart was keen to find something that would repeat the success of *Die Entführung* and da Ponte was an accomplished poet. Opera was perhaps Mozart's favourite form of self-expression: he enjoyed

The Imperial Palace in Vienna

Illustration to *The Magic Flute*

the spectacle and the action, and particularly liked comedy and wit. He liked to act the fool and had even appeared in a pantomime for the Vienna carnival with Aloysia and Joseph Lange in 1783.

He had written two unfinished comic operas over the last two years but had put them aside. One of the plays he knew was Beaumarchais' *Le Mariage de Figaro* (The Marriage of Figaro) and this sprang to mind as a theme for da Ponte to develop. The plot, whereby an intelligent servant outwits his inferior master, Count Almaviva, preventing him from carrying out his wicked schemes, was clearly one that appealed. It also has its darker side, as where the Countess laments her husband's infidelities, and the fact that he no longer seems to love her. The women characters are also independent, carrying out their own successful stratagem to force the men to behave. All of this was quite novel at the time, and seen as deeply subversive, as it implied that the unravelling of the *ancien regime*, the old system, was long overdue (the French Revolution took place only three years later, in 1789). The structure of the plot enabled Mozart to make full use of his musical versatility, colouring the different moods and emotions. The first performance was given on 1 May 1786. It did not meet with universal applause in Vienna because of its political implications (the play itself had not been allowed to be performed). Salieri was thought to be jealous of Mozart because the Emperor had given Mozart special permission to put it on. Prague, which was to prove itself the city most in sympathy with Mozart, was rapturous. The political aspects of the plot particularly appealed to it. But more important for Mozart, the orchestra, the true connoisseurs, broke into applause during the first full rehearsal after the aria '*Non piu andrai*'.

Mozart did receive a small commission for the Emperor's fête at Schönbrunn, for which Salieri also wrote a festive piece. Mozart's piece was a short opera, *Der Schauspieldirektor* (The Impresario), about an opera producer's difficulties with rival prima donnas in mounting an opera, something of which he had some experience. But he was having mounting difficulties keeping his hectic life going. He had to move pupils to the afternoon to leave the mornings free for composing, as he desperately tried to earn money from new pieces for public concerts (the piano concertos in A major (K 488), No. 23, and in C minor (K 491), No 24). At the end of 1787 he went to Prague, where he was amazed to find tunes from *Figaro* being sung in the streets. This was a small ray of light in the dark years that remained to him.

Years of Struggle

When Mozart returned from Prague in early
1787, he had a new commission in his
pocket, for *Don Giovanni*. But shortly after
his return, in March, Leopold died. Mozart
must have had very mixed feelings about
this: while in some respects, Leopold had
been tyrannical, controlling the minutiae of
Mozart's life, he had been a good mentor,
and he had acted out of concern for his son.
Now he was no longer available in any
capacity. Mozart fell back on the principles
of Freemasonry (he had become a Mason at

Mozart receives the commission for the *Requiem*

Wolfgang Amadeus Mozart

the end of 1784), which were to be stoical, showing a brave face to the world in the midst of troubles.

Other close friends had died at roughly the same time, and Mozart began to feel increasingly lonely. But meanwhile he had to work on *Don Giovanni*. He worked closely with da Ponte, fine tuning every word. Unlike in his other operas, his sympathies clearly lie with the Don himself, who is an unredeemed scoundrel, but at the same time full of humour and indisputably brave. Here the devil clearly has the best tunes. The forces of good are feeble; at no point are they able to best Don Giovanni, or even his servant Leporello. The only force that can do that is the supernatural, which comes right at the end of the opera to drag the Don to hell. The supernatural takes the form of a living statue, that of the Commendatore, whom the Don had killed early in the story. He is clearly another awesome and unsympathetic authority figure. The overture is grim and foreboding, with a seriousness that none of the other operas have. Mozart perhaps let feelings of depression slip as he penned it. And despite the humour, it has some of the most sombre – frightening almost – music that he ever wrote. The premiere was in Prague on 29 October. Its reception was very enthusiastic.

By summer 1788 Mozart was deep in debt. In June he had to move back to the suburbs to save money. His first daughter, Theresa, born only the previous Christmas, died ten days after the move. Although three of his operas were being performed in Vienna, they did not bring in much money. *Don Giovanni* was not popular there and only played fifteen times, never to do so again in Mozart's lifetime. Meanwhile Austria declared war on Turkey. Mozart wrote a few patriotic songs to take advantage of this but they did not pay particularly well. He also offered for subscription three string quintets (K 406, 515 and 516) written in 1787, to try and repay one of his main creditors – and friend – Johann Puchberg. But he was always behind, reduced to embarrassedly begging Puchberg for more. He also performed in public: the 'Coronation' Piano Concerto (K 537), No. 26, seems to have been written with such an aim. It lacks the strength of the 20th, for example, or the soulfulness of the 27th (K 595).

But despite his problems Mozart was highly productive, writing his three last symphonies during the summer. He finished No. 39 in E flat (K 543) on 26 June, No. 40 in G minor on 25 July, and No. 41 in C major (K 551), 'The Jupiter', on 10 August. These works tower above their predecessors: the E flat symphony is perhaps the most powerful, using the full range of orchestral colours, whereas there are no trumpets or drums in the G minor and no clarinets in the C major. The opening of the E flat is Beethovenian in weight and majesty. These great symphonies, though, were almost certainly not performed while he was still alive. So they cannot have brought in any money. However, in November Mozart appeared as conductor and arranger at a concert of Handel's work organized by his friend Van Swieten. This must have paid quite well as Mozart shortly afterwards moved back into central Vienna.

1789 brought new worries. Constanze began to be ill. She was only twenty-seven but had had four children during her marriage and was pregnant with a fifth. Mozart for the first time travelled without her, when he visited Prague to conduct his re-orchestration of Handel's *Messiah*. He clearly missed her badly; this is indicated by the number of letters he wrote, and his comment that he looked at her portrait every morning and night. She did not seem to return his feelings, which must have hurt such a sensitive person as Mozart. And in 1789 he travelled extensively. Prince Karl Lichnowsky, a pupil and fellow Mason, invited Mozart to accompany him to Dresden. Mozart had high hopes of receiving work from this tour. (He had to borrow more money to finance this trip.) At Dresden he played before the Elector Frederick Augustus, improvising on the organ that J. S. Bach had used at St Thomas's Church. He then went on to Leipzig for a financially disastrous public concert. Lichnowsky disappeared at this point having actually borrowed money off Mozart.

After this he visited Frederick William II, King of Prussia, at the latter's invitation. Mozart wrote variations on the King's favourite piece of music and was rewarded with a small sum of money and two commissions: for six easy piano sonatas for the king's daughter and for six quartets. He returned to Vienna on 4 June, warning Constanze that she would have to be pleased to see him if not any money. He immediately began work on the first of what are now known as the 'Prussian' Quartets, in D major (K 575). He clearly did not find the work very inspiring as he used themes from earlier works and had to give undue prominence to the cello, the King's instrument. For all that, the work is pleasant and sunny.

Another subscription concert organized by Van Swieten was an abject failure: Van Swieten was the sole subscriber. And Constanze was growing worse. The Mozarts' physician advised that she go for a cure to Baden. This meant finding more money. Swallowing his pride, Mozart called again on Puchberg; understandably the latter was slow to reply, but eventually sent 150 gulden. Constanze and Mozart then went to Baden, Mozart leaving after a few days. Back in Vienna, he worked on new arias for a revival of *The Marriage of Figaro*. This was successful and Joseph II commissioned a new opera. This and the money from Puchberg seemed to have unlocked his creativity: not only did he write the wonderful Clarinet Quintet (K 581), but he also composed *Cosi fan Tutte* (Thus Do All Women – i.e. behave like this). *Cosi* is subtitled the 'School for Lovers'. Essentially the plot is that the lovers of two sisters pretend to go off to the wars and then return in disguise to try and seduce their friend's fiancée. Both men are successful in this underhand exercise, though this leads to much bad blood between them. Finally the impostors are to marry the other's fiancée, but then all is revealed and the original couples reform. None of the characters, men or women, come out in a good light. The opera is often described as cynical, unlike *Marriage of Figaro*, but in reality what it does is explode the over-sentimentality of much romance. In December 1789, Mozart was rehearsing it, and it was premiered on 26 January 1790. It was well-received but only had five performances because on 20 February 1790 – Mozart cannot be said at any point to have been particularly lucky – Joseph II died, and the theatres had to close for a period of mourning.

The harder tone of this opera may have something to do both with Mozart's financial situation and his unhappiness with Constanze's behaviour at Baden. She had always been flirtatious, and rumours reached him that she was being so with a vengeance. His faith in human nature must have been severely tried, as she was one of the few people remaining to whom he felt close. His creativity almost dried up completely in 1790; his personal record of works he wrote that year is almost empty – two more 'Prussian' Quartets (K 589 and K 590) and an arrangement of some Handel for Van Swieten. He looked around for more pupils but seems to have only found two, when he could have taken up to eight. One of these was Franz Xaver Süssmayr, who took lessons in composition and theory, and who was later to complete the *Requiem*. In the autumn Mozart planned a tour as a performer; Leopold II was due to be crowned Holy Roman Emperor in Frankfurt in the autumn. On his journey Mozart encountered many old acquaintances – his last trip there had been in 1763, as a child prodigy. But he was clearly unhappy: he shunned company, which was out of character, and found everything cold, 'ice-cold', he wrote to Constanze. Tears were falling on the paper as he wrote.

In Frankfurt he was dogged by bad luck.
Salieri had accompanied the Emperor, and
none of Mozart's compositions were to be
performed. A performance of *Don Giovanni*
was cancelled and replaced by an opera by
Dittersdorf. His hopes of earning a decent
sum of money were dashed. He decided to
head back for Vienna, via Mannheim, where
Figaro was produced, and Munich, where
Karl Theodor persuaded him to linger and
play. He bypassed Salzburg and Nannerl,
who lived close by, opting instead for
Linz, with its happier memories. He was
back in Vienna in November, back to the
apartment in which he was to spend his
remaining days. He received an invitation
from the London impresario, Robert
O'Reilly, to come to London for six
months, from December 1790 to June
1791, with a commission for two operas,
paying £300 – a considerable sum. We do
not know how or if he replied, but how

differently things might have turned out if he had accepted. Given Haydn's impact in London in 1791, how much more success might Mozart have enjoyed, with the financial security and better health that goes with it.

In December 1790 Mozart met Haydn for the last time at a farewell dinner: Haydn was 58 and Mozart sadly reflected that he would never see him again. He never did but that was not because Haydn died.

The Final Year

Mozart's last year was one of unparalleled creativity, during which he produced some of his greatest and most haunting works – the *Ave Verum* (K 614), *Die Zauberflöte* (The Magic Flute), *La Clemenza di Tito* (The Mercy of Titus), and the Clarinet Concerto in A major (K 622).

On 4 March 1791 he gave his last concert performance: Mozart found public performances draining and promised Constanze to cease giving them. At this concert, he almost certainly played his last piano concerto, No. 27 in B flat major (K 595), which he had completed on 4 January. This work has an other-worldly quality that some say suggests a premonitory awareness of impending death. Constanze was pregnant again, and needed to go to Baden once more in the early summer for the sake of her health. It is a mark of Mozart's desperation that he applied for and received the post of unpaid assistant to the *Kapellmeister* in Vienna, hoping to receive a salary when the aged incumbent died. In the event, the man outlived Mozart.

He took even the most trivial commissions, including some for mechanical organs, and wrote several dances, rather more effective than his father's efforts. More important, though, he began to discuss with his friend, Emanuel Schikaneder, the idea of producing an opera together. Schikaneder was manager of the Theater auf der Wieden (the suburb in which Mozart had lived) and specialised in putting on semi-comic populist operas, often with a strong element of pantomime. Mozart went several times to the auf der Wieden and had a clear idea of what Schikaneder would want. The result was *Die Zauberflöte*.

The opera has been noted for its Masonic elements: Mozart seemed to regard Masonry as an alternative religion, and the themes of love only successfully being achieved through purification by ordeal and the triumph of humanism over material considerations shine through the slapstick. Sarastro, the king-priest- magician figure, has some of Mozart's noblest music. Mozart conducted the first performance on 30 September. In many ways it was the opera he most loved, attending on several occasions (and sometimes mischievously playing the glockenspiel – musical bells – offstage). Salieri saw and praised it, and Mozart lived long enough to see it become a great success, having had over twenty-four performances by mid-November. Ironically, it was to be his first major success in Vienna – and the last.

He also received the commission for the *Requiem (K 626)*. Romantic myths about this commission abound: it is true that Mozart did not know from whom the commission originated as it came via inter-mediaries. In fact it was from a friend of Puchberg, a Count Walsegg, who wanted to pass the composition off as his own. We shall never know if the appearance of a black-clad servant, as if an agent of the Devil, frightened Mozart to death. It appears unlikely, given that he was simultaneously composing music with much humour in it, despite his troubles. It is curious, though, that while he had the creative energy to finish *Die Zauberflöte*, he was unable to finish the *Requiem*, and also failed to finish the C minor mass. It is as if he found orthodox religion, with its patriarchal aspect, and his memories of Colloredo, more of a duty than an inspiration.

Over the last summer of his life, hope drained away as the endless busy round of life, the endless scrabbling for money, his loneliness with Constanze away at Baden, the belief that the future would be no better, wore away his natural optimism. But having started the year with barely any work on the horizon, while he was still composing *Die Zauberflöte* in July he received the commission for *La Clemenza di Tito*. This was to be performed at the coronation of the Emperor Leopold II as King of Bohemia, in Prague in September.

La Clemenza is a reversion to the now totally outdated *opera seria* form. The subject matter is the attempt to murder Tito (the Roman Emperor Titus), by Sesto (Sextus), a close friend of his, who has been inveigled into the attempt by Vitellia, who is bitter because she thinks Tito will not choose her as Empress. In the event, she is wrong, but too late to stop the machinery of assassination. The Capitol is burnt down but Sesto misses his mark and wounds somebody else. Vitellia finally confesses that she is the chief conspirator: Tito forgives her and releases Sesto. The themes of jealousy and betrayal dominate the opera: there is nobility in forgiveness, but the guilty, if of good character, like Sesto, can never forgive themselves.

His true elegy seems to have been in the Clarinet Concerto, which has the serenity of one who has looked death in the face and not been frightened. The *Requiem*, while very powerful, has an impersonal feel. It is very sombre and any sense of redemption is not exultant.

The last piece of music he completed was a cantata, '*Laut verkünde unsre Freude*' – 'Loudly, we announce our joy' (K 623) – written to celebrate the opening of new premises for his Masonic lodge. Its title somewhat dispels the myths, partially fabricated by Constanze, of the misery of his last few weeks. He recorded its completion on 15 November and conducted it on the 18th. It was that evening, probably, that he felt the first symptoms of a chill.

It turned out to be more serious: on 20 November he took to his bed and a doctor was sent for. His joints began to swell with the rheumatism that had troubled him as a child. He may too have had a kidney infection, which often shows through swelling. Much contemporary medicine contained arsenic which would have aggravated any such infection. His doctor, Closset, who was an expert in this field, recognized the seriousness of the illness and on 28 November called in another specialist. Mozart was conscious all the time, if feverish. He only had one important unfinished commission, the *Requiem*. On Saturday 3 November his fever grew worse. Sophie Weber came the following morning (it is from her account written several years later that we know) and Mozart pleaded with her to stay, to see him die. Sophie then went for a priest, and while she was away, some friends came to Mozart's apartment to rehearse the *Requiem*. When they reached '*Lacrimosa dies illa*' – 'That day of weeping' – Mozart burst into tears and could not go further. When Sophie returned, after the others had gone, she found him explaining to Süssmayr how to complete the *Requiem*. Mozart began to experience a burning sensation in his head; Sophie sent for Closset, who was eventually tracked down at the theatre. He advised the application of cold compresses to his head. Sophie applied them, but the shock sent Mozart into a coma. Midnight came and it was now Monday 5 December. Just under an hour into the new day, he drew his last breath.

Mozart's poverty was evident from the meagre possessions that he left his widow, the only luxury being a billiards table. Neither Constanze nor other of his apparently closest friends accompanied his coffin to its burial. His coffin was placed in an unmarked grave. It is not surprising that when Constanze eventually went to look for it seventeen years later, she could not find it. Vienna ignored its greatest adoptive son, apart from Mozart's Masonic lodge, which conducted an oration. Only Prague, the scene of his greatest triumphs, a city which reciprocated his affection, did him the honour of a full requiem mass.